CW00969828

Ecclesiastes
Teacher of Realism

ECCLESIASTES, TEACHER OF REALISM
© Copyright Scandinavia Publishing House
Nørregade 32, DK-1165 Copenhagen K, Denmark
Tel. 01-14 00 91

Edited by Jørgen Vium Olesen
Graphic design by Otto Wikkelsø

Bible text from *The Holy Bible, International Version*,
copyright New York International Bible Society.
Used by permission.

Printed in Hong Kong by South Sea International Press Ltd.

ISBN 87 7247 164 6

Ecclesiastes

Teacher of Realism

Edited by Jørgen Vium Olesen

Illustrated for Daily Meditation

Scandinavia

Preface

By many the Book of Ecclesiastes has been regarded as the ultimate expression of pessimism: From the opening paragraph to the end of the book the Teacher is exposing his audience to the utter futility of a life based upon earthly ambitions and desires. Any world view which does not rise above the horizon of man himself is doomed to meaninglessness and frustration. With the sharp pen of a philosopher in the ancient wisdom tradition, who has tried out all the pleasures and virtues of human life, he concludes with appalling clarity that "Everything is Meaningless!" However in the midst of this analysis of the vanity in human life there is one significant exception to complete futility: as a mere creature man only derives importance from his relationship to the almighty Creator. Therefore: "Remember your Creator in the days of your youth!" From this perspective the book changes from being a book of *pessimism* to a book of *realism*. Let it speak meditatively to you and adhere to its exhortation — before you encounter the grave, the ultimate expression of futility!

**"Meaningless! Meaningless!"
says the Teacher.
"Utterly meaningless!
Everything is meaningless."**

Ecclesiastes 1:2

He has made everything beautiful
in its time. He has also set
eternity in the hearts of men;
yet they cannot fathom what God
has done from beginning to end.

Ecclesiastes 3:11

Everything is Meaningless

The words of the Teacher, son of David,
  king in Jerusalem:
"Meaningless! Meaningless!"
  says the Teacher.
"Utterly meaningless!
  Everything is meaningless."
What does man gain from all his labor
  at which he toils under the sun??
Generations come and generations go,
  but the earth remains forever.
The sun rises and the sun sets,
  and hurries back to where it rises.
The wind blows to the south
  and turns to the north;
round and round it goes,
  ever returning on its course.
All streams flow into the sea,
  yet the sea is never full.
To the place the streams come from,
  there they return again.
All things are wearisome,
  more than one can say.
The eye never has enough of seeing,
  or the ear its fill of hearing.
What has been will be again,
  what has been done will be done again;
  there is nothing new under the sun.
Is there anything of which one can say,
  "Look! This is something new?"
It was here already, long ago;
  it was here before our time.
There is no remembrance of men of old,
  and even those who are yet to come
will not be remembered by those who follow.

Generations come and generations go,
  but the earth remains forever.

Wisdom

I, the Teacher,
  was king over Israel in Jerusalem.
I devoted myself to study and to explore
  by wisdom all that is done under heaven.
What a heavy burden
  God has laid on men!
I have seen all the things
  that are done under the sun;
  all of them are meaningless,
a chasing after the wind.
What is twisted cannot be straightened;
  what is lacking cannot be counted.
I thought to myself, "Look, I have
  grown and increased in wisdom
  more than anyone who has ruled
  over Jerusalem before me;
I have experienced much of wisdom
  and knowledge."
Then I applied myself to
  the understanding of wisdom,
  and also of madness and folly,
  but I learned that this, too,
  is a chasing after the wind.
For with much wisdom comes much sorrow;
  the more knowledge, the more grief.

I have seen all the things
  that are done under the sun;
  all of them are meaningless,
  a chasing after the wind.

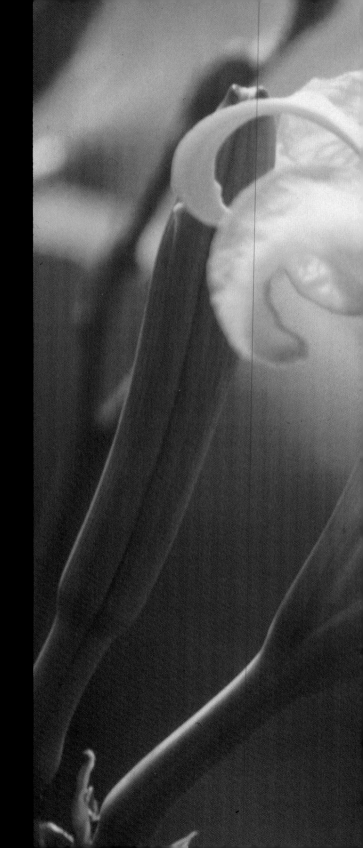

Pleasures

I thought in my heart, "Come now,
  I will test you with pleasure
  to find out what is good." But that also proved
  to be meaningless.
"Laughter," I said, "is foolish.
  And what does pleasure accomplish?"
I tried cheering myself with wine,
  and embracing folly — my mind still
  guiding me with wisdom. I wanted to see what
  was worthwhile for men to do under heaven
  during the few days of their lives.
I undertook great projects: I built houses for
  myself and planted vineyards. I made gardens
  and parks and planted all kinds of fruit trees
  in them.
I made reservoirs to water groves of flourishing
  trees. I bought male and female slaves and had
  other slaves who were born in my house.
I also owned more herds and flocks than anyone
  in Jerusalem before me. I amassed silver
  and gold for myself, and the treasure of kings
  and provinces.
I acquired men and women singers,
  and a harem as well — the delights
  of the heart of man.
I became greater by far than anyone in
  Jerusalem before me. In all this my wisdom
  stayed with me.
I denied myself nothing my eyes desired;
  I refused my heart no pleasure.
My heart took delight in all my work,
  and this was the reward for all my labor.
Yet when I surveyed all that my hands had done
  and what I had toiled to achieve,
everything was meaningless,
  a chasing after the wind;
  nothing was gained under the sun.

I undertook great projects: I built houses
  for myself and planted vineyards.
I made gardens and parks and planted
  all kinds of fruit trees in them.

Ecclesiastes 2:12,16

The Wise and the Fool
— All the Same

Then I turned my thoughts to consider wisdom,
  and also madness and folly.
What more can the king's successor do
  than what has already been done?
I saw that wisdom is better than folly,
  just as light is better than darkness.
The wise man has eyes in his head,
  while the fool walks in the darkness;
but I came to realize that the same fate
  overtakes them both.
  Then I thought in my heart,
"The fate of the fool will overtake me also.
  What then do I gain by being wise?"
I said in my heart,
  "This too is meaningless."
For the wise man, like the fool,
  will not be long remembered;
  in days to come both will be forgotten.
Like the fool, the wise man too must die!

The wise man has eyes in his head,
  while the fool walks in the darkness;
but I came to realize that the same fate
  overtakes them both.

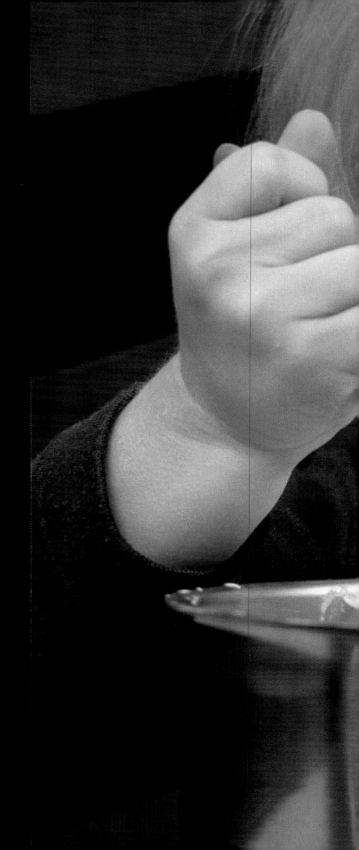

Toil

So I hated life, because the work that is done
under the sun was grievous to me.
All of it is meaningless, a chasing after the wind.
I hated all the things I had toiled for
under the sun, because I must leave them
to the one who comes after me.
And who knows whether he will be a wise man
or a fool?
Yet he will have control over all the work
into which I have poured my effort and skill
under the sun. This too is meaningless.
So my heart began to despair over all
my toilsome labor under the sun.
For a man may do his work with wisdom,
knowledge and skill, and then he must leave all
he owns to someone who has not worked for it.
This too is meaningless and a great misfortune.
What does a man get for all the toil and anxious
striving with which he labors under the sun?
All his days his work is pain and grief;
even at night his mind does not rest.
This too is meaningless.
A man can do nothing better than to eat
and drink and find satisfaction in his work.
This too, I see, is from the hand of God,
for without him, who can eat or find
enjoyment?
To the man who pleases him,
God gives wisdom, knowledge and happiness,
but to the sinner he gives the task of gathering
and storing up wealth to hand it over to the one
who pleases God.
This too is meaningless, a chasing after the wind.

A man can do nothing better than to eat
and drink and find satisfaction in his work.
This too, I see, is from the hand of God,
for without him, who can eat or find
enjoyment?

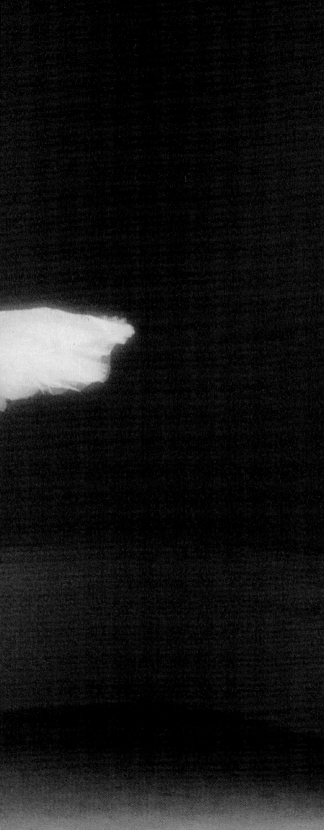

A Time for Everything

There is a time for everything,
and a season for every activity under heaven:
a time to be born and a time to die,
a time to plant and a time to uproot
a time to kill and a time to heal,
a time to tear down and a time to build,
a time to weep and a time to laugh,
a time to mourn and a time to dance,
a time to scatter stones and a time
  to gather them,
a time to embrace and a time to refrain,
a time to search and a time to give up,
a time to keep and a time to throw away,
a time to tear and a time to mend,
a time to be silent and a time to speak,
a time to love and a time to hate,
a time for war and a time for peace.

A time to mourn and a time to dance...

Eternity in Their Hearts

What does the worker gain from his toil?
  I have seen the burden God has laid on men.
He has made everything beautiful in its time.
He has also set eternity in the hearts of men;
  yet they cannot fathom what God has done
  from beginning to end.
I know that there is nothing better for men
  than to be happy and do good while they live.
That every man may eat and drink,
  and find satisfaction in all his toil —
  this is the gift of God.
I know that everything God does will endure
  forever; nothing can be added to it and nothing
  taken from it. God does it,
  so men will revere him.
Whatever is has already been,
  and what will be has been before;
  and God will call the past to account.

*I know that everything God does
  will endure forever; nothing can be added
  to it and nothing taken from it.
  God does it, so men will revere him.*

There is a time for everything,
and a season for every activity
under heaven:
a time to be born and a time
to die, time to plant
and a time to uproot.

Ecclesiastes 3:1

Ecclesiastes 3:16-22

From Dust to Dust

And I saw something else under the sun:
In the place of judgment — wickedness was there,
  in the place of justice — wickedness was there.
I thought in my heart,
"God will bring to judgment
  both the righteous and the wicked,
for there will be a time for every activity,
  a time for every deed."
I also thought, "As for men,
  God tests them so that they may see
  that they are like the animals.
Man's fate is like that of the animals;
  the same fate awaits them both: As one dies,
  so dies the other.
All have the same breath; man has no advantage
  over the animal. Everything is meaningless.
All go to the same place; all come from dust,
  and to dust all return.
Who knows if the spirit of man rises upward
  and if the spirit of the animal goes down
  into the earth?"
So I saw that there is nothing better
  for a man than to enjoy his work,
  because that is his lot.
For who can bring him to see what will
  happen after him?

All go to the same place; all come from dust,
and to dust all return.

Oppression

Again I looked and saw all the oppression
  that was taking place under the sun:
I saw the tears of the oppressed —
  and they have no comforter;
power was on the side of the oppressors —
  and they have no comforter.
And I declared that the dead,
  who had already died,
are happier than the living,
  who are still alive.
But better than both
  is he who has not yet been,
who has not seen the evil
  that is done under the sun.
And I saw that all labor, and all achievement
  spring from man's envy of his neighbor.
  This too is meaningless,
  a chasing after the wind.
The fool folds his hands
  and ruins himself.
Better one handful with tranquillity
  than two handfuls with toil
  and chasing after the wind.

I saw the tears of the oppressed —
  and they have no comforter;
power was on the side of the oppressors —
  and they have no comforter.

Ecclesiastes 4:7-12

Two Are Better Than One

Again I saw something meaningless
  under the sun:
There was a man all alone;
  he had neither son nor brother.
There was no end to his toil,
  yet his eyes were not content with his wealth.
"For whom am I toiling," he asked,
  "and why am I depriving myself
  of enjoyment?"
This too is meaningless —
  a miserable business!
Two are better than one,
  because they have a good return
  for their work:
If one falls down,
  his friend can help him up.
But pity the man who falls
  and has no one to help him up!
Also, if two lie down together,
  they will keep warm.
  But how can one keep warm alone?
Though one may be overpowered,
  two can defend themselves.
A cord of three strands is not quickly broken.

Two are better than one,
  because they have a good return
  for their work:
If one falls down,
  his friend can help him up.

Give Heed to a Warning

Better a poor but wise youth
  than an old but foolish king
  who no longer knows how to take warning.
The youth may have come from prison to the
  kingship, or he may have been born in poverty
  within his kingdom.
I saw that all who lived and walked
  under the sun followed the youth,
  the king's successor.
There was no end to all the people
  who were before them.
  But those who came later were not pleased
  with the successor.
This too is meaningless, a chasing after the wind.

Better a poor but wise youth
  than an old but foolish king
  who no longer knows how to take warning.

Consider Your Words

Guard your steps when you go to the house
  of God.
Go near to listen rather than to offer the sacrifice
  of fools, who do not know that they do wrong.
Do not be quick with your mouth,
  do not be hasty in your heart
  to utter anything before God.
God is in heaven
  and you are on earth,
  so let your words be few.
As a dream comes when there are many cares,
  so the speech of a fool
  when there are many words.
When you make a vow to God, do not delay
  in fulfilling it. He has no pleasure in fools;
  fulfill your vow.
It is better not to vow than to make a vow
  and not fulfill it.
Do not let your mouth lead you into sin.
  And do not protest to the temple messenger,
"My vow was a mistake." Why should God
  be angry at what you say and destroy the work
  of your hands?
Much dreaming and many words are
  meaningless.
Therefore stand in awe of God.

When you make a vow to God, do not delay
  in fulfilling it. He has no pleasure in fools;
  fulfill your vow.

Riches

If you see the poor oppressed in a district,
  and justice and rights denied,
  do not be surprised at such things;
for one official is eyed by a higher one,
  and over them both are others higher still.
The increase from the land is taken by all;
  the king himself profits from the fields.
Whoever loves money never has money enough;
  whoever loves wealth is never satisfied
  with his income.
  This too is meaningless.
As goods increase,
  so do those who consume them.
And what benefit are they to the owner
  except to feast his eyes on them?
The sleep of the laborer is sweet,
  whether he eats little or much,
but the abundance of a rich man
  permits him no sleep.

The sleep of the laborer is sweet,
  whether he eats little or much,
but the abundance of a rich man
  permits him no sleep.

A Grievous Evil

I have seen another evil under the sun,
  and it weighs heavily on men:
God gives a man wealth,
  possessions and honor, so that he
  lacks nothing his heart desires,
  but God does not enable him to enjoy them,
  and a stranger enjoys them instead.
This is meaningless, a grievous evil.
A man may have a hundred children
  and live many years;
yet no matter how long he lives,
  if he cannot enjoy his prosperity and does not
  receive proper burial,
I say that a stillborn child is better off than he.
  It comes without meaning,
  it departs in darkness,
  and in darkness its name is shrouded.
Though it never saw the sun or knew anything,
  it has more rest than does that man
  — even if he lives a thousand years twice over
  but fails to enjoy his prosperity.
Do not all go to the same place?

God gives a man wealth,
  possessions and honor, so that he
  lacks nothing his heart desires,
  but God does not enable him to enjoy them,
  and a stranger enjoys them instead.
This is meaningless, a grievous evil.

Who Can Tell?

All man's efforts are for his mouth,
  yet his appetite is never satisfied.
What advantage has a wise man
  over a fool?
What does a poor man gain
  by knowing how to conduct himself
  before others?
Better what the eye sees
  than the roving of the appetite.
This too is meaningless,
  a chasing after the wind.
Whatever exists has already been named,
  and what man is has been known;
no man can contend
  with one who is stronger than he.
The more the words,
  the less the meaning,
  and how does that profit anyone?
For who knows what is good for a man in life,
  during the few and meaningless days
  he passes through like a shadow?
Who can tell him what will happen
  under the sun after he is gone?

For who knows what is good for a man in life,
  during the few and meaningless days
  he passes through like a shadow?
Who can tell him what will happen
  under the sun after he is gone?

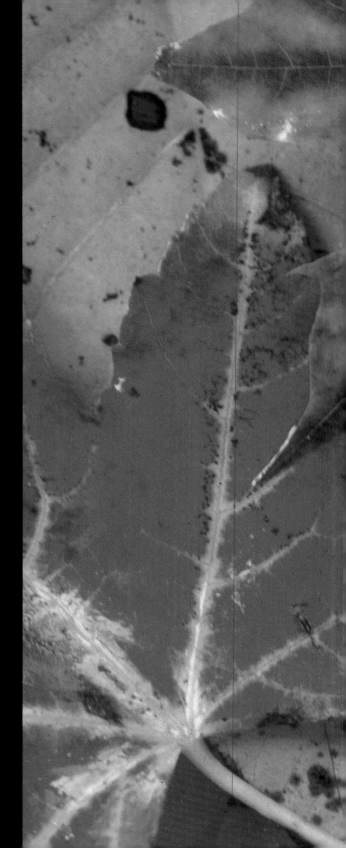

Destiny

A good name is better than fine perfume,
  and the day of death better than the day of birth.
It is better to go to a house of mourning
  than to go to a house of feasting,
for death is the destiny of every man;
  the living should take this to heart.
Sorrow is better than laughter,
  because a sad face is good for the heart.
The heart of the wise is in the house of mourning,
  but the heart of fools is in the house of pleasure.
It is better to heed a wise man's rebuke
  than to listen to the song of fools.
Like the crackling of thorns under the pot,
  so is the laughter of fools.
  This too is meaningless.
Extortion turns a wise man into a fool,
  and a bribe corrupts the heart.
The end of a matter is better than its beginning,
  and patience is better than pride.
Do not be quickly provoked in your spirit,
  for anger resides in the lap of fools.

Death is the destiny of every man;
  the living should take this to heart.

Realism

Do not say, "Why were the old days better
  than these?"
  For it is not wise to ask such questions.
Wisdom, like an inheritance, is a good thing
  and benefits those who see the sun.
Wisdom is a shelter,
  as money is a shelter,
but the advantage of knowledge is this:
  that wisdom preserves the life of its possessor.
Consider what God has done:
Who can straighten
  what he has made crooked?
When times are good, be happy;
  but when times are bad, consider.
God has made the one
  as well as the other.
Therefore, a man cannot discover
  anything about his future.
In this meaningless life of mine
  I have seen both of these:
a righteous man perishing in his righteousness,
  and a wicked man living long in his wickedness.
Do not be overrighteous,
  neither be overwise —
  why destroy yourself?
Do not be overwicked,
  and do not be a fool —
  why die before your time?
It is good to grasp the one
  and not let go of the other.
  The man who fears God will avoid
  all extremes.
Wisdom makes one wise man more powerful
  than ten rulers in a city.
There is not a righteous man on earth
  who does what is right and never sins.
Do not pay attention to every word people say,
  or you may hear your servant cursing you —
for you know in your heart
  that many times you yourself
  have cursed others.

Do not be overrighteous,
  neither be overwise —
  why destroy yourself?

The Smooth Made Crooked

All this I tested by wisdom and I said,
"I am determined to be wise" —
  but this was beyond me,
Whatever wisdom may be,
  it is far off and most profound —
  who can discover it?
So I turned my mind to understand,
  to investigate and to search out wisdom
  and the scheme of things
and to understand the stupidity of wickedness
  and the madness of folly.
I find more bitter than death
  the woman who is a snare,
whose heart is a trap
  and whose hands are chains.
The man who pleases God will escape her,
  but the sinner she will ensnare.
"Look," says the Teacher,
  "this is what I have discovered:
"Adding one thing to another to discover
  the scheme of things —
  while I was still searching
  but not finding —
I found one upright man among a thousand,
  but not one upright woman among them all.
This only have I found:
  God made mankind upright,
  but men have gone in search
  of many schemes."

This only have I found:
  God made mankind upright,
but men have gone in search
  of many schemes.

Obedience

Who is like the wise man?
Who knows the explanation of things?
Wisdom brightens a man's face
  and changes its hard appearance.
Obey the king's command, I say, because you
  took an oath before God.
Do not be in a hurry to leave the king's
  presence.
Do not stand up for a bad cause,
  for he will do whatever he pleases.
Since a king's word is supreme,
  who can say to him, "What are you doing?"
Whoever obeys his command
  will come to no harm,
  and the wise heart will know
  the proper time and procedure.
For there is a proper time and procedure
  for every matter,
  though a man's misery weighs heavily
  upon him.
Since no man knows the future,
  who can tell him what is to come?
No man has power over the wind to contain it;
  so no one has power over the day of his death.
As no one is discharged time of war,
  so wickedness will not release
  those who practice it.

No man has power over the wind to contain it;
so no one has power over the day of his death.

Fearing God Is Better

All this I saw, as I applied my mind
  to everything under the sun.
There is a time when a man lords it over others
  to his own hurt.
Then too, I saw the wicked buried
  — those who used to come and go from
  the holy place and receive praise in the city
  where they did this.
This too is meaningless.
When the sentence for a crime
  is not quickly carried out,
  the hearts of the people are filled with schemes
  to do wrong.
Although a wicked man commits
  a hundred crimes and still lives a long time,
I know that it will go better
  with God-fearing men,
  who are reverent before God.
Yet because the wicked do not fear God,
  it will not go well with them,
and their days will not lengthen like a shadow.

All this I saw, as I applied my mind
  to everything under the sun.
There is a time when a man
  lords it over others to his own hurt.

**This only have I found:
God made mankind
upright,
but men have gone
in search of many
schemes.**

Ecclesiastes 7:29

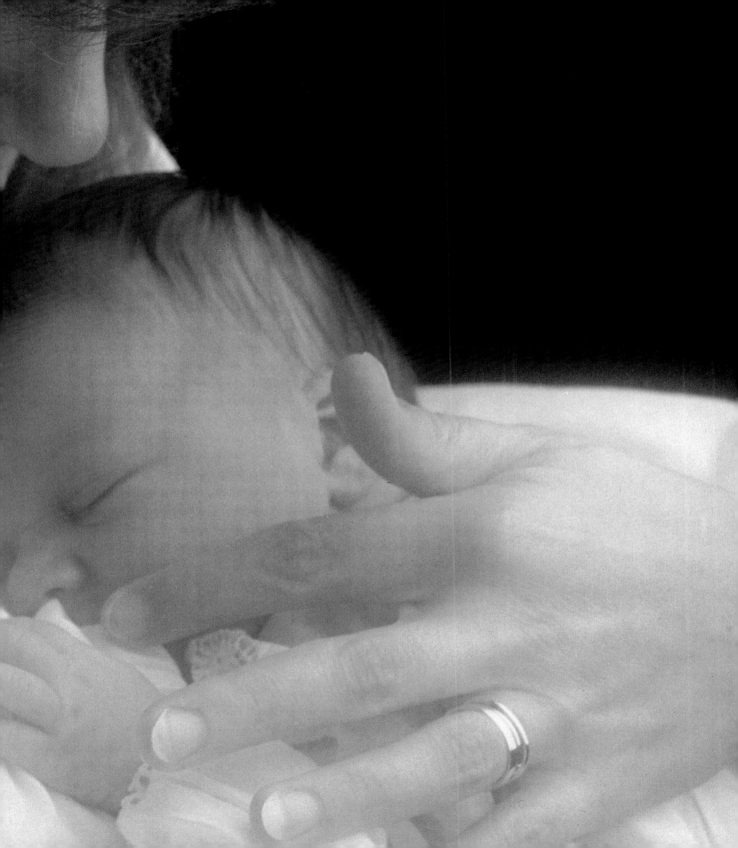

Inscrutable

There is something else meaningless
  that occurs on earth:
    righteous men who get what the wicked
    deserve, and wicked men who get
    what the righteous deserve.
This too, I say, is meaningless.
So I commend the enjoyment of life,
  because nothing is better for a man
  under the sun than to eat and drink
  and be glad.
Then joy will accompany him in his work all
  the days of the life God has given him
  under the sun.
When I applied my mind to know wisdom
  and to observe man's labor on the earth
    — his eyes not seeing sleep day or night
    — then I saw all that God has done.
No one can comprehend what goes on
  under the sun.
Despite all his efforts to search it out,
  man cannot discover its meaning.
Even if a wise man claims he knows,
  he cannot really comprehend it.

No one can comprehend what goes on
  under the sun.
Despite all his efforts to search it out,
  man cannot discover its meaning.
Even if a wise man claims he knows,
  he cannot really comprehend it.

A Common Destiny
for Everybody

So I reflected on all this and concluded
  that the righteous and the wise
  and what they do are in God's hands,
  but no man knows whether love or hate
  awaits him.
All share a common destiny — the righteous
  and the wicked, the good and the bad,
  the clean and the unclean, those who offer
  sacrifices and those who do not.
As it is with the good man,
  so with the sinner;
as it is with those who take oaths,
  so with those who are afraid to take them.
This is the evil in everything that happens
  under the sun:
The same destiny overtakes all.
The hearts of men, moreover, are full of evil
  and there is madness in their hearts
  while they live, and afterward
  they join the dead.
Anyone who is among the living has hope
  — even a live dog is better off than a dead lion!
For the living know that they will die,
  but the dead know nothing;
they have no further reward,
  and even the memory of them is forgotten.
Their love, their hate
  and their jealousy have long since vanished;
never again will they have a part
  in anything that happens under the sun.
Go, eat your food with gladness,
  and drink your wine with a joyful heart,
  for it is now that God favors what you do.
Always be clothed in white,
  and always anoint your head with oil.

Go, eat your food with gladness,
  and drink your wine with a joyful heart,
  for it is now that God favors what you do.
Always be clothed in white,
  and always anoint your head with oil.

Ecclesiastes 9:9-12

Therefore...

Enjoy life with your wife, whom you love,
  all the days of this meaningless life
  that God has given you under the sun
  — all your meaningless days.
For this is your lot in life and in your
  toilsome labor under the sun.
Whatever your hand finds to do,
  do it with all your might, for in the grave,
  where you are going, their is neither working
  nor planning nor knowledge nor wisdom.
I have seen something else under the sun:
The race is not to the swift
  or the battle to the strong,
nor does food come to the wise
  or wealth to the brilliant
  or favor to the learned;
but time and chance happen to them all.
Moreover, no man knows when his hour
  will come:
As fish are caught in a cruel net,
  or birds are taken in a snare,
so men are trapped by evil times
  that fall unexpectedly upon them.

Moreover, no man knows when his hour
  will come:
As fish are caught in a cruel net,
  or birds are taken in a snare,
so men are trapped by evil times
  that fall unexpectedly upon them.

Wisdom Better Than Folly

I also saw under the sun this example of wisdom
  that greatly impressed me:
There was once a small city
  with only a few people in it.
And a powerful king came against it,
  surrounded it and built huge siegeworks against it.
Now there lived in that city a man poor but wise,
  and he saved the city by his wisdom.
  But nobody remembered that poor man.
So I said, "Wisdom is better than strength."
  But the poor man's wisdom is despised,
  and his words are no longer heeded.
The quiet words of the wise are more to be heeded
  than the shouts of a ruler of fools.
Wisdom is better than weapons of war,
  but one sinner destroys much good.

The quiet words of the wise
  are more to be heeded
  than the shouts of a ruler of fools.
Wisdom is better than weapons of war,
  but one sinner destroys much good.

Wisdom in Action

As dead flies give perfume a bad smell,
　so a little folly outweighs wisdom and honor.
The heart of the wise inclines to the right,
　but the heart of the fool to the left.
Even as he walks along the road,
　the fool lacks sense
　and shows everyone how stupid he is.
If a ruler's anger rises against you,
　do not leave your post;
　calmness can lay great errors to rest.
There is an evil I have seen under the sun,
　the sort of error that arises from a ruler:
Fools are put in many high positions,
　while the rich occupy the low ones.
I have seen slaves on horseback,
　while princes go on foot like slaves.
Whoever digs a pit may fall into it;
　whoever breaks through a wall may be bitten
　by a snake.
Whoever quarries stones may be injured
　by them;
　whoever splits logs may be endangered
　by them.
If the axe is dull and its edge unsharpened,
　more strength is needed
　but skill will bring success.
If a snake bites before it is charmed,
　there is no profit for the charmer.

If the axe is dull and its edge unsharpened,
*　more strength is needed*
*　but skill will bring success.*

Words, Words, Words...

Words from a wise man's mouth are gracious,
  but a fool is consumed by his own lips.
At the beginning his words are folly;
  at the end they are wicked madness —
  and the fool multiplies words.
No one knows what is coming —
  who can tell him what will happen after him?
A fool's work wearies him;
  he does not know the way to town.
Woe to you, O land whose king was a servant
  and whose princes feast in the morning.
Blessed are you, O land whose king is
  of noble birth
  and whose princes eat at a proper time —
  for strength and not for drunkenness.
If a man if lazy, the rafters sag;
  if his hands are idle, the house leaks.
A feast is made for laughter,
  and wine makes life merry,
  but money is the answer for everything.
Do not revile the king even in your thoughts,
  or curse the rich in your bedroom,
because a bird of the air may carry your words,
  and a bird on the wing may report
  what you say.

Do not revile the king even in your thoughts,
  or curse the rich in your bedroom,
because a bird of the air may carry
  your words, and a bird on the wing
  may report what you say.

Greater is He!

Cast your bread upon the waters,
  for after many days you will find it again.
Give portions to seven, yes to eight,
  for you do not know what disaster
  may come upon the land.
If clouds are full of water,
  they pour rain upon the earth.
Whether a tree falls to the south or to the north,
  in the place where it falls, there will it lie.
Whoever watches the wind will not plant;
  whoever looks at the clouds will not reap.
As you do not know the path of the wind,
  or how the body is formed in a mother's womb,
so you cannot understand the work of God,
  the Maker of all things.
Sow your seed in the morning,
  and at evening let not your hands be idle,
for you do not know which will succeed,
  whether this or that,
  or whether both will do equally well.

As you do not know the path of the wind,
  or how the body is formed in a mother's womb,
so you cannot understand the work of God,
  the Maker of all things.

Enjoy life with your wife,
  whom you love, all the days
  of this meaningless life
  that God has given you
  under the sun
  — all your meaningless days.
For this is your lot in life
  and in your toilsome labor
  under the sun.

Ecclesiastes 9:9

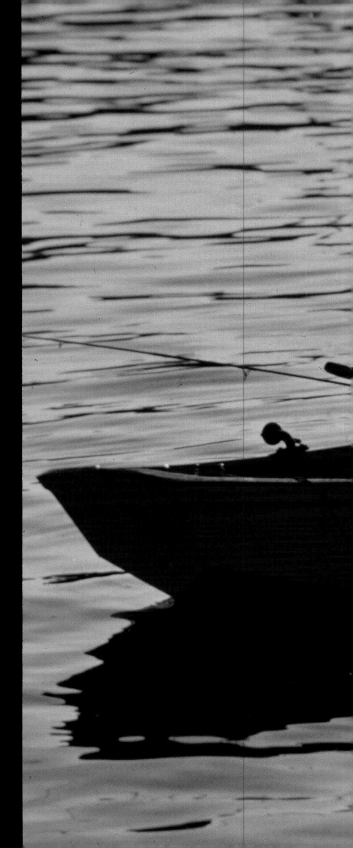

Remember Your Creator

Light is sweet,
  and it pleases the eyes to see the sun.
However many years a man may live,
  let him enjoy them all.
But let him remember the days of darkness,
  for they will be many.
  Everything to come is meaningless.
Be happy, young man, while you are young,
  and let your heart give you joy
  in the days of your youth.
Follow the ways of your heart
  and whatever your eyes see,
but know that for all these things
  God will bring you to judgment.
So then, banish anxiety from your heart
  and cast off the troubles of your body,
  for youth and vigor are meaningless.

Be happy, young man, while you are young,
  and let your heart give you joy
  in the days of your youth.

Remember your Creator!

Remember your Creator
  in the days of your youth,
before the days of trouble come
  and the years approach when you will say,
  "I find no pleasure in them" —
before the sun and the light
  and the moon and the stars grow dark,
  and the clouds return after the rain;
when the keepers of the house tremble,
  and the strong men stoop,
when the grinders cease because they are few,
  and those looking through the windows
  grow dim;
when the doors to the street are closed
  and the sound of grinding fades;
when men rise up at the sound of birds,
  but all their songs grow faint;
when men are afraid of heights
  and of dangers in the streets;
when the almond tree blossoms
  and the grasshopper drags himself along
  and desire no longer is stirred.
Then man goes to his eternal home
  and mourners go about the streets.
Remember him — before the silver cord
  is severed,
  or the golden bowl is broken;
before the pitcher is shattered at the spring,
  or the wheel broken at the well,
and the dust returns to the ground it came from,
  and the spirit returns to God who gave it.
"Meaningless! Meaningless!" says the Teacher.
"Everything is meaningless!"

Remember him — before the silver cord
  is severed,
  or the golden bowl is broken;
before the pitcher is shattered at the spring,
  or the wheel broken at the well,
and the dust returns to the ground
  it came from,
  and the spirit returns to God who gave it.

The Conclusion of the Matter

Not only was the Teacher wise,
  but also he imparted knowledge to the people.
He pondered and searched out
  and set in order many proverbs.
The Teacher searched to find
  just the right words, and what he wrote
  was upright and true.
The words of the wise are like goads,
  their collected sayings like firmly embedded
  nails — given by one Shepherd.
Be warned, my son, of anything
  in addition to them.
Of making many books there is no end,
  and much study wearies the body.
Now all has been heard;
  here is the conclusion of the matter:
Fear God and keep his commandments,
  for this is the duty of man.
For God will bring every deed into judgment,
  including every hidden thing,
  whether it is good or evil.

Fear God and keep his commandments,
  for this is the duty of man.
For God will bring every deed into judgment,
  including every hidden thing,
  whether it is good or evil.

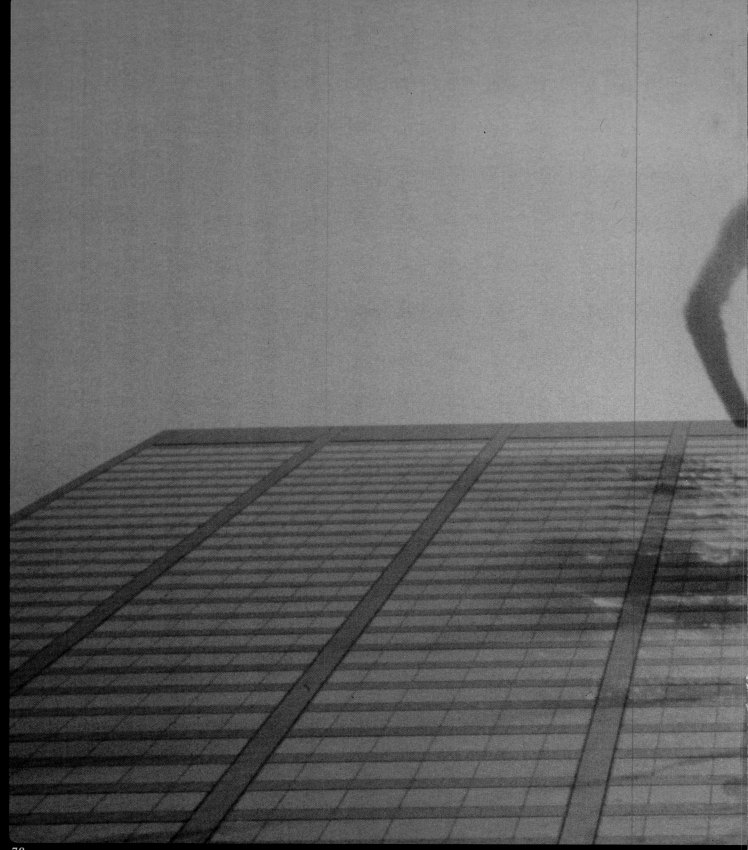

Remember you Creator
in the days of your youth,
before the days of trouble come
and the years approach
when you will say,
"I find no pleasure in them."

Ecclesiastes 12:1

Be happy, young man, while you are young,
and let your heart give you joy
in the days of your youth.
Follow the ways of your heart and
whatever your eyes see,
but know that for all these things
God will bring you to judgment